POPE FRANCIS

Patris Corde

Apostolic Letter
on the 150ᵗʰ Anniversary
of the Proclamation of Saint Joseph
as Patron of the Universal Church

In Appendix
YEAR OF SAINT JOSEPH
Decree of the Apostolic Penitentiary
Saint Joseph and the Popes
Prayers to the Saint

LIBRERIA
EDITRICE
VATICANA

Appendix edited by Giuseppe Merola
Translated in English by Helen Crombie

Cover Image:
Sleeping Saint Joseph
Hand-painted ceramic statue
Artist: Brunella Malfatti
Photo © Libreria Editrice Vaticana

ISBN 978-88-266-0564-7

www.vatican.va

www.libreriaeditricevaticana.com

POPE FRANCIS

Apostolic Letter

Patris Corde

on the 150th Anniversary
of the Proclamation of Saint Joseph
as Patron of the Universal Church

WITH A FATHER'S HEART: that is how Joseph loved Jesus, whom all four Gospels refer to as *"the son of Joseph"*.[1]

Matthew and Luke, the two Evangelists who speak most of Joseph, tell us very little, yet enough for us to appreciate what sort of father he was, and the mission entrusted to him by God's providence.

---

[1] *Lk* 4:22; *Jn* 6:42; cf. *Mt* 13:55; *Mk* 6:3.

We know that Joseph was a lowly carpenter (cf. *Mt* 13:55), betrothed to Mary (cf. *Mt* 1:18; *Lk* 1:27). He was a "just man" (*Mt* 1:19), ever ready to carry out God's will as revealed to him in the Law (cf. *Lk* 2:22.27.39) and through four dreams (cf. *Mt* 1:20; 2:13.19.22). After a long and tiring journey from Nazareth to Bethlehem, he beheld the birth of the Messiah in a stable, since "there was no place for them" elsewhere (cf. *Lk* 2:7). He witnessed the adoration of the shepherds (cf. *Lk* 2:8-20) and the Magi (cf. *Mt* 2:1-12), who represented respectively the people of Israel and the pagan peoples.

Joseph had the courage to become the legal father of Jesus, to whom he gave the name revealed by the angel: "You shall call his name Jesus, for he will save his people from their sins" (*Mt* 1:21). As we know, for ancient peoples, to give a name to a person or to a thing, as Adam did in the account in the Book of Genesis (cf. 2:19-20), was to establish a relationship.

In the Temple, forty days after Jesus' birth, Joseph and Mary offered their child to the Lord and listened with amazement to Simeon's prophecy concerning Jesus and his Mother (cf. *Lk* 2:22-35). To protect Jesus from Herod, Joseph dwelt as a foreigner in

Egypt (cf. *Mt* 2:13-18). After returning to his own country, he led a hidden life in the tiny and obscure village of Nazareth in Galilee, far from Bethlehem, his ancestral town, and from Jerusalem and the Temple. Of Nazareth it was said, "No prophet is to rise" (cf. *Jn* 7:52) and indeed, "Can anything good come out of Nazareth?" (cf. *Jn* 1:46). When, during a pilgrimage to Jerusalem, Joseph and Mary lost track of the twelve-year-old Jesus, they anxiously sought him out and they found him in the Temple, in discussion with the doctors of the Law (cf. *Lk* 2:41-50).

After Mary, the Mother of God, no saint is mentioned more frequently in the papal magisterium than Joseph, her spouse. My Predecessors reflected on the message contained in the limited information handed down by the Gospels in order to appreciate more fully his central role in the history of salvation. Blessed Pius IX declared him "Patron of the Catholic Church",[2] Venerable Pius XII proposed him as "Patron of Workers"[3] and Saint John Paul

[2] S. RITUUM CONGREGATIO, *Quemadmodum Deus* (8 December 1870): *ASS* 6 (1870-71), 194.

[3] Cf. *Address to ACLI on the Solemnity of Saint Joseph the Worker* (1 May 1955): *AAS* 47 (1955), 406.

II as "Guardian of the Redeemer".[4] Saint Joseph is universally invoked as the "patron of a happy death".[5]

Now, one hundred and fifty years after his proclamation as *Patron of the Catholic Church* by Blessed Pius IX (8 December 1870), I would like to share some personal reflections on this extraordinary figure, so close to our own human experience. For, as Jesus says, "out of the abundance of the heart the mouth speaks" (*Mt* 12:34). My desire to do so increased during these months of pandemic, when we experienced, amid the crisis, how "our lives are woven together and sustained by ordinary people, people often overlooked. People who do not appear in newspaper and magazine headlines, or on the latest television show, yet in these very days are surely shaping the decisive events of our history. Doctors, nurses, storekeepers and supermarket workers, cleaning personnel, caregivers, transport workers, men and women working to provide essential services and public safety, volunteers, priests, men and women

[4] Cf. Apostolic Exhortation *Redemptoris Custos* (15 August 1989): *AAS* 82 (1990), 5-34.

[5] *Catechism of the Catholic Church*, 1014.

religious, and so very many others. They understood that no one is saved alone… How many people daily exercise patience and offer hope, taking care to spread not panic, but shared responsibility. How many fathers, mothers, grandparents and teachers are showing our children, in small everyday ways, how to accept and deal with a crisis by adjusting their routines, looking ahead and encouraging the practice of prayer. How many are praying, making sacrifices and interceding for the good of all".[6] Each of us can discover in Joseph – the man who goes unnoticed, a daily, discreet and hidden presence – an intercessor, a support and a guide in times of trouble. Saint Joseph reminds us that those who appear hidden or in the shadows can play an incomparable role in the history of salvation. A word of recognition and of gratitude is due to them all.

1. *A beloved father*

The greatness of Saint Joseph is that he was the spouse of Mary and the father of Jesus. In this way, he placed himself, in the words of Saint John Chrys-

[6] *Meditation in the Time of Pandemic* (27 March 2020): *L'Osservatore Romano*, 29 March 2020, p. 10.

ostom, "at the service of the entire plan of salvation".[7]

Saint Paul VI pointed out that Joseph concretely expressed his fatherhood "by making his life a sacrificial service to the mystery of the incarnation and its redemptive purpose. He employed his legal authority over the Holy Family to devote himself completely to them in his life and work. He turned his human vocation to domestic love into a superhuman oblation of himself, his heart and all his abilities, a love placed at the service of the Messiah who was growing to maturity in his home".[8]

Thanks to his role in salvation history, Saint Joseph has always been venerated as a father by the Christian people. This is shown by the countless churches dedicated to him worldwide, the numerous religious Institutes, Confraternities and ecclesial groups inspired by his spirituality and bearing his name, and the many traditional expressions of piety in his honour. Innumerable holy men and women were passionately devoted to him. Among them was

[7] *In Matthaeum Homiliae*, V, 3: PG 57, 58.
[8] *Homily* (19 March 1966): *Insegnamenti di Paolo VI*, IV (1966), 110.

Teresa of Avila, who chose him as her advocate and intercessor, had frequent recourse to him and received whatever graces she asked of him. Encouraged by her own experience, Teresa persuaded others to cultivate devotion to Joseph.[9]

Every prayer book contains prayers to Saint Joseph. Special prayers are offered to him each Wednesday and especially during the month of March, which is traditionally dedicated to him.[10]

Popular trust in Saint Joseph is seen in the expression *"Go to Joseph"*, which evokes the famine in Egypt, when the Egyptians begged Pharaoh for bread. He in turn replied: "Go to Joseph; what he says to you, do" (*Gen* 41:55). Pharaoh was refer-

---

[9] Cf. *Autobiography*, 6, 6-8.

[10] Every day, for over forty years, following Lauds I have recited a prayer to Saint Joseph taken from a nineteenth-century French prayer book of the Congregation of the Sisters of Jesus and Mary. It expresses devotion and trust, and even poses a certain challenge to Saint Joseph: "Glorious Patriarch Saint Joseph, whose power makes the impossible possible, come to my aid in these times of anguish and difficulty. Take under your protection the serious and troubling situations that I commend to you, that they may have a happy outcome. My beloved father, all my trust is in you. Let it not be said that I invoked you in vain, and since you can do everything with Jesus and Mary, show me that your goodness is as great as your power. Amen."

ring to Joseph the son of Jacob, who was sold into slavery because of the jealousy of his brothers (cf. *Gen* 37:11-28) and who – according to the biblical account – subsequently became viceroy of Egypt (cf. *Gen* 41:41-44).

As a descendant of David (cf. *Mt* 1:16-20), from whose stock Jesus was to spring according to the promise made to David by the prophet Nathan (cf. *2 Sam* 7), and as the spouse of Mary of Nazareth, Saint Joseph stands at the crossroads between the Old and New Testaments.

2. *A tender and loving father*

Joseph saw Jesus grow daily "in wisdom and in years and in divine and human favour" (*Lk* 2:52). As the Lord had done with Israel, so Joseph did with Jesus: he taught him to walk, taking him by the hand; he was for him like a father who raises an infant to his cheeks, bending down to him and feeding him (cf. *Hos* 11:3-4).

In Joseph, Jesus saw the tender love of God: "As a father has compassion for his children, so the Lord has compassion for those who fear him" (*Ps* 103:13).

In the synagogue, during the praying of the Psalms, Joseph would surely have heard again and again that the

God of Israel is a God of tender love,[11] who is good to all, whose "compassion is over all that he has made" (*Ps* 145:9).

The history of salvation is worked out "in hope against hope" (*Rom* 4:18), through our weaknesses. All too often, we think that God works only through our better parts, yet most of his plans are realized in and despite our frailty. Thus Saint Paul could say: "To keep me from being too elated, a thorn was given me in the flesh, a messenger of Satan to torment me, to keep me from being too elated. Three times I appealed to the Lord about this, that it would leave me, but he said to me: 'My grace is sufficient for you, for power is made perfect in weakness'" (*2 Cor* 12:7-9).

Since this is part of the entire economy of salvation, we must learn to look upon our weaknesses with tender mercy.[12]

The evil one makes us see and condemn our frailty, whereas the Spirit brings it to light with tender love. Tenderness is the best way to touch

[11] Cf. *Deut* 4:31; *Ps* 69:16; 78:38; 86:5; 111:4; 116:5; *Jer* 31:20.

[12] Cf. Apostolic Exhortation *Evangelii Gaudium* (24 November 2013), 88, 288: *AAS* 105 (2013), 1057, 1136-1137.

the frailty within us. Pointing fingers and judging others are frequently signs of an inability to accept our own weaknesses, our own frailty. Only tender love will save us from the snares of the accuser (cf. *Rev* 12:10). That is why it is so important to encounter God's mercy, especially in the Sacrament of Reconciliation, where we experience his truth and tenderness. Paradoxically, the evil one can also speak the truth to us, yet he does so only to condemn us. We know that God's truth does not condemn, but instead welcomes, embraces, sustains and forgives us. That truth always presents itself to us like the merciful father in Jesus' parable (cf. *Lk* 15:11-32). It comes out to meet us, restores our dignity, sets us back on our feet and rejoices for us, for, as the father says: "This my son was dead and is alive again; he was lost and is found" (v. 24).

Even through Joseph's fears, God's will, his history and his plan were at work. Joseph, then, teaches us that faith in God includes believing that he can work even through our fears, our frailties and our weaknesses. He also teaches us that amid the tempests of life, we must never be afraid to let the Lord steer our course. At times, we want to be in complete control, yet God always sees the bigger picture.

3. *An obedient father*

As he had done with Mary, God revealed his saving plan to Joseph. He did so by using dreams, which in the Bible and among all ancient peoples, were considered a way for him to make his will known.[13]

Joseph was deeply troubled by Mary's mysterious pregnancy. He did not want to "expose her to public disgrace",[14] so he decided to "dismiss her quietly" (*Mt* 1:19).

In the first dream, an angel helps him resolve his grave dilemma: "Do not be afraid to take Mary as your wife, for the child conceived in her is from the Holy Spirit. She will bear a son, and you are to name him Jesus, for he will save his people from their sins" (*Mt* 1:20-21). Joseph's response was immediate: "When Joseph awoke from sleep, he did as the angel of the Lord commanded him" (*Mt* 1:24). Obedience

[13] Cf. *Gen* 20:3; 28:12; 31:11.24; 40:8; 41:1-32; *Num* 12:6; *1 Sam* 3:3-10; *Dan* 2, 4; *Job* 33:15.

[14] In such cases, provisions were made even for stoning (cf. *Deut* 22:20-21).

made it possible for him to surmount his difficulties and spare Mary.

In the second dream, the angel tells Joseph: "Get up, take the child and his mother, and flee to Egypt, and remain there until I tell you; for Herod is about to search for the child, to destroy him" (*Mt* 2:13). Joseph did not hesitate to obey, regardless of the hardship involved: "He got up, took the child and his mother by night, and went to Egypt, and remained there until the death of Herod" (*Mt* 2:14-15).

In Egypt, Joseph awaited with patient trust the angel's notice that he could safely return home. In a third dream, the angel told him that those who sought to kill the child were dead and ordered him to rise, take the child and his mother, and return to the land of Israel (cf. *Mt* 2:19-20). Once again, Joseph promptly obeyed. "He got up, took the child and his mother, and went to the land of Israel" (*Mt* 2:21).

During the return journey, "when Joseph heard that Archelaus was ruling over Judea in place of his father Herod, he was afraid to go there. After being warned in a dream" – now for the fourth time – "he went away to the district of Galilee. There he made his home in a town called Nazareth" (*Mt* 2:22-23).

The evangelist Luke, for his part, tells us that Joseph undertook the long and difficult journey from Nazareth to Bethlehem to be registered in his family's town of origin in the census of the Emperor Caesar Augustus. There Jesus was born (cf. *Lk* 2:7) and his birth, like that of every other child, was recorded in the registry of the Empire. Saint Luke is especially concerned to tell us that Jesus' parents observed all the prescriptions of the Law: the rites of the circumcision of Jesus, the purification of Mary after childbirth, the offering of the firstborn to God (cf. 2:21-24).[15]

In every situation, Joseph declared his own "fiat", like those of Mary at the Annunciation and Jesus in the Garden of Gethsemane.

In his role as the head of a family, Joseph taught Jesus to be obedient to his parents (cf. *Lk* 2:51), in accordance with God's command (cf. *Ex* 20:12).

During the hidden years in Nazareth, Jesus learned at the school of Joseph to do the will of the Father. That will was to be his daily food (cf. *Jn* 4:34). Even at the most difficult moment of his life, in Gethsemane, Jesus chose to do the Father's

---

[15] Cf. *Lev* 12:1-8; *Ex* 13:2.

will rather than his own,[16] becoming "obedient unto death, even death on a cross" (*Phil* 2:8). The author of the Letter to the Hebrews thus concludes that Jesus "learned obedience through what he suffered" (5:8).

All this makes it clear that "Saint Joseph was called by God to serve the person and mission of Jesus directly through the exercise of his fatherhood" and that in this way, "he cooperated in the fullness of time in the great mystery of salvation and is truly a minister of salvation."[17]

4. *An accepting father*

Joseph accepted Mary unconditionally. He trusted in the angel's words. "The nobility of Joseph's heart is such that what he learned from the law he made dependent on charity. Today, in our world where psychological, verbal and physical violence towards women is so evident, Joseph appears as the figure of a respectful and sensitive man. Even though he does not understand the bigger picture, he makes a

[16] Cf. *Mt* 26:39; *Mk* 14:36; *Lk* 22:42.
[17] SAINT JOHN PAUL II, Apostolic Exhortation *Redemptoris Custos* (15 August 1989), 8: *AAS* 82 (1990), 14.

decision to protect Mary's good name, her dignity and her life. In his hesitation about how best to act, God helped him by enlightening his judgment".[18]

Often in life, things happen whose meaning we do not understand. Our first reaction is frequently one of disappointment and rebellion. Joseph set aside his own ideas in order to accept the course of events and, mysterious as they seemed, to embrace them, take responsibility for them and make them part of his own history. Unless we are reconciled with our own history, we will be unable to take a single step forward, for we will always remain hostage to our expectations and the disappointments that follow.

The spiritual path that Joseph traces for us is not one that *explains*, but *accepts*. Only as a result of this acceptance, this reconciliation, can we begin to glimpse a broader history, a deeper meaning. We can almost hear an echo of the impassioned reply of Job to his wife, who had urged him to rebel against the evil he endured: "Shall we receive the good at the hand of God, and not receive the bad?" (*Job* 2:10).

[18] *Homily at Mass and Beatifications*, Villavicencio, Colombia (8 September 2017): *AAS* 109 (2017), 1061.

Joseph is certainly not passively resigned, but courageously and firmly proactive. In our own lives, acceptance and welcome can be an expression of the Holy Spirit's gift of fortitude. Only the Lord can give us the strength needed to accept life as it is, with all its contradictions, frustrations and disappointments.

Jesus' appearance in our midst is a gift from the Father, which makes it possible for each of us to be reconciled to the flesh of our own history, even when we fail to understand it completely.

Just as God told Joseph: "Son of David, do not be afraid!" (*Mt* 1:20), so he seems to tell us: "Do not be afraid!" We need to set aside all anger and disappointment, and to embrace the way things are, even when they do not turn out as we wish. Not with mere resignation but with hope and courage. In this way, we become open to a deeper meaning. Our lives can be miraculously reborn if we find the courage to live them in accordance with the Gospel. It does not matter if everything seems to have gone wrong or some things can no longer be fixed. God can make flowers spring up from stony ground. Even if our heart condemns us, "God is greater than our hearts, and he knows everything" (*1 Jn* 3:20).

Here, once again, we encounter that Christian realism which rejects nothing that exists. Reality, in its mysterious and irreducible complexity, is the bearer of existential meaning, with all its lights and shadows. Thus, the Apostle Paul can say: "We know that all things work together for good, for those who love God" (*Rom* 8:28). To which Saint Augustine adds, "even that which is called evil (*etiam illud quod malum dicitur*)".[19] In this greater perspective, faith gives meaning to every event, however happy or sad.

Nor should we ever think that believing means finding facile and comforting solutions. The faith Christ taught us is what we see in Saint Joseph. He did not look for shortcuts, but confronted reality with open eyes and accepted personal responsibility for it.

Joseph's attitude encourages us to accept and welcome others as they are, without exception, and to show special concern for the weak, for God chooses what is weak (cf. *1 Cor* 1:27). He is the "Father of orphans and protector of widows" (*Ps* 68:6), who commands us to love the stranger in our midst.[20] I

---

[19] *Enchiridion de fide, spe et caritate*, 3.11: PL 40, 236.
[20] Cf. *Deut* 10:19; *Ex* 22:20-22; *Lk* 10:29-37.

like to think that it was from Saint Joseph that Jesus drew inspiration for the parable of the prodigal son and the merciful father (cf. *Lk* 15:11-32).

5. *A creatively courageous father*

If the first stage of all true interior healing is to accept our personal history and embrace even the things in life that we did not choose, we must now add another important element: creative courage. This emerges especially in the way we deal with difficulties. In the face of difficulty, we can either give up and walk away, or somehow engage with it. At times, difficulties bring out resources we did not even think we had.

As we read the infancy narratives, we may often wonder why God did not act in a more direct and clear way. Yet God acts through events and people. Joseph was the man chosen by God to guide the beginnings of the history of redemption. He was the true "miracle" by which God saves the child and his mother. God acted by trusting in Joseph's creative courage. Arriving in Bethlehem and finding no lodging where Mary could give birth, Joseph took a stable and, as best he could, turned it into a welcoming home for the Son of God come into the world (cf. *Lk* 2:6-7). Faced with imminent danger from Herod, who wanted to kill the child, Joseph was warned once again in a dream to protect the child, and rose in the middle of the night to prepare the flight into Egypt (cf. *Mt* 2:13-14).

A superficial reading of these stories can often give the impression that the world is at the mercy of the strong and mighty, but the "good news" of the Gospel consists in showing that, for all the arrogance and violence of worldly powers, God always finds a way to carry out his saving plan. So too, our lives may at times seem to be at the mercy of the powerful, but the Gospel shows us what counts. God always finds a way to save us, provided we show the same creative courage as the carpenter of Nazareth, who was able to turn a problem into a possibility by trusting always in divine providence.

If at times God seems not to help us, surely this does not mean that we have been abandoned, but instead are being trusted to plan, to be creative, and to find solutions ourselves.

That kind of creative courage was shown by the friends of the paralytic, who lowered him from the roof in order to bring him to Jesus (cf. *Lk* 5:17-26). Difficulties did not stand in the way of those friends' boldness and persistence. They were convinced that Jesus could heal the man, and "finding no way to bring him in because of the crowd, they went up on the roof and let him down with his bed through the tiles into the middle of the crowd in front of Jesus. When he saw their faith, he said, 'Friend, your sins are forgiven you'" (vv. 19-20). Jesus recognized the creative faith with which they sought to bring their sick friend to him.

The Gospel does not tell us how long Mary, Joseph and the child remained in Egypt. Yet they certainly needed to eat, to find a home and employment. It does not take much imagination to fill in those details. The Holy Family had to face concrete problems like every other family, like so many of our migrant brothers and sisters who, today too, risk their lives to escape misfortune and hunger. In this regard, I consider Saint Joseph the special patron of all those forced to leave their native lands because of war, hatred, persecution and poverty.

At the end of every account in which Joseph plays a role, the Gospel tells us that he gets up, takes the child and his mother, and does what God commanded him (cf. *Mt* 1:24; 2:14.21). Indeed, Jesus and

Mary his Mother are the most precious treasure of our faith.[21]

In the divine plan of salvation, the Son is inseparable from his Mother, from Mary, who "advanced in her pilgrimage of faith, and faithfully persevered in her union with her Son until she stood at the cross".[22]

We should always consider whether we ourselves are protecting Jesus and Mary, for they are also mysteriously entrusted to our own responsibility, care and safekeeping. The Son of the Almighty came into our world in a state of great vulnerability. He needed to be defended, protected, cared for and raised by Joseph. God trusted Joseph, as did Mary, who found in him someone who would not only save her life, but would always provide for her and her child. In this sense, Saint Joseph could not be other than the Guardian of the Church, for the Church is the continuation of the Body of Christ in history, even as Mary's motherhood is reflected in

[21] Cf. S. RITUUM CONGREGATIO, *Quemadmodum Deus* (8 December 1870): *ASS* 6 (1870-1871), 193; BLESSED PIUS IX, Apostolic Letter *Inclytum Patriarcham* (7 July 1871): l.c., 324-327.

[22] SECOND VATICAN ECUMENICAL COUNCIL, Dogmatic Constitution on the Church *Lumen Gentium*, 58.

the motherhood of the Church.[23] In his continued protection of the Church, Joseph continues to protect *the child and his mother*, and we too, by our love for the Church, continue to love *the child and his mother*.

That child would go on to say: "As you did it to one of the least of these who are members of my family, you did it to me" (*Mt* 25:40). Consequently, every poor, needy, suffering or dying person, every stranger, every prisoner, every infirm person is "the child" whom Joseph continues to protect. For this reason, Saint Joseph is invoked as protector of the unfortunate, the needy, exiles, the afflicted, the poor and the dying. Consequently, the Church cannot fail to show a special love for the least of our brothers and sisters, for Jesus showed a particular concern for them and personally identified with them. From Saint Joseph, we must learn that same care and responsibility. We must learn to love the child and his mother, to love the sacraments and charity, to love the Church and the poor. Each of these realities is always *the child and his mother*.

---

[23] *Catechism of the Catholic Church*, 963-970.

6. *A working father*

An aspect of Saint Joseph that has been emphasized from the time of the first social Encyclical, Pope Leo XIII's *Rerum Novarum*, is his relation to work. Saint Joseph was a carpenter who earned an honest living to provide for his family. From him, Jesus learned the value, the dignity and the joy of what it means to eat bread that is the fruit of one's own labour.

In our own day, when employment has once more become a burning social issue, and unemployment at times reaches record levels even in nations that for decades have enjoyed a certain degree of prosperity, there is a renewed need to appreciate the importance of dignified work, of which Saint Joseph is an exemplary patron.

Work is a means of participating in the work of salvation, an opportunity to hasten the coming of the Kingdom, to develop our talents and abilities, and to put them at the service of society and fraternal communion. It becomes an opportunity for the fulfilment not only of oneself, but also of that primary cell of society which is the family. A family without work is particularly vulnerable to difficulties, tensions, estrangement and even break-up. How can we speak of human dignity without working to ensure that everyone is able to earn a decent living?

Working persons, whatever their job may be, are cooperating with God himself, and in some way become creators of the world around us. The crisis of our time, which is economic, social, cultural and spiritual, can serve as a summons for all of us to rediscover the value, the importance and necessity of work for bringing about a new "normal" from which no one is excluded. Saint Joseph's work reminds us that God himself, in becoming man, did not disdain work. The loss of employment that affects so many of our brothers and sisters, and has increased as a result of the Covid-19 pandemic, should serve as a summons to review our priorities. Let us implore Saint Joseph the Worker to help us find ways to express our firm conviction that no young person, no person at all, no family should be without work!

7. *A father in the shadows*

The Polish writer Jan Dobraczyński, in his book *The Shadow of the Father*,[24] tells the story of Saint Joseph's life in the form of a novel. He uses

[24] Original edition: *Cień Ojca*, Warsaw, 1977.

the evocative image of a shadow to define Joseph. In his relationship to Jesus, Joseph was the earthly shadow of the heavenly Father: he watched over him and protected him, never leaving him to go his own way. We can think of Moses' words to Israel: "In the wilderness... you saw how the Lord your God carried you, just as one carries a child, all the way that you travelled" *(Deut* 1:31). In a similar way, Joseph acted as a father for his whole life.[25]

Fathers are not born, but made. A man does not become a father simply by bringing a child into the world, but by taking up the responsibility to care for that child. Whenever a man accepts responsibility for the life of another, in some way he becomes a father to that person.

Children today often seem orphans, lacking fathers. The Church too needs fathers. Saint Paul's words to the Corinthians remain timely: "Though you have countless guides in Christ, you do not have many fathers" *(1 Cor* 4:15). Every priest or bishop should be able to add, with the Apostle: "I became your father in Christ Jesus through the Gospel" (ibid.). Paul likewise calls the Galatians: "My little

[25] Cf. SAINT JOHN PAUL II, Apostolic Exhortation *Redemptoris Custos*, 7-8: *AAS* 82 (1990), 12-16.

children, with whom I am again in travail until Christ be formed in you!" (4:19).

Being a father entails introducing children to life and reality. Not holding them back, being over-protective or possessive, but rather making them capable of deciding for themselves, enjoying freedom and exploring new possibilities. Perhaps for this reason, Joseph is traditionally called a "most chaste" father. That title is not simply a sign of affection, but the summation of an attitude that is the opposite of possessiveness. Chastity is freedom from possessiveness in every sphere of one's life. Only when love is chaste, is it truly love. A possessive love ultimately becomes dangerous: it imprisons, constricts and makes for misery. God himself loved humanity with a chaste love; he left us free even to go astray and set ourselves against him. The logic of love is always the logic of freedom, and Joseph knew how to love with extraordinary freedom. He never made himself the centre of things. He did not think of himself, but focused instead on the lives of Mary and Jesus.

Joseph found happiness not in mere self-sacrifice but in self-gift. In him, we never see frustration but only trust. His patient silence was the prelude to concrete expressions of trust. Our world today needs fathers. It has no use for tyrants who would domineer others as a means of compensating for their own needs. It rejects those who confuse authority with authoritarianism, service with servility, discussion with oppression, charity with a welfare mentality, power with destruction. Every true vocation is born of the gift of oneself, which is the fruit of mature sacrifice. The priesthood and consecrated life likewise require this kind of maturity. Whatever our vocation, whether to marriage, celibacy or virginity, our gift of self will not come to fulfilment if it stops at sacrifice; were that the case, instead of becoming a sign of the beauty and joy of love, the gift of self would risk being an expression of unhappiness, sadness and frustration.

When fathers refuse to live the lives of their children for them, new and unexpected vistas open up. Every child is the bearer of a unique mystery that can only be brought to light with the help of a father who respects that child's freedom. A father who realizes that he is most a father and educator at the point when he becomes "useless", when he sees that his child has become independent and can walk the paths of life unaccompanied. When he becomes like Joseph, who always knew that his child was not his own but had merely been entrusted to his care. In the end, this is what Jesus would have us understand when he says: "Call no man your father on earth, for you have one Father, who is in heaven" (*Mt* 23:9).

In every exercise of our fatherhood, we should always keep in mind that it has nothing to do with possession, but is rather a "sign" pointing to a greater fatherhood. In a way, we are all like Joseph: a shadow of the heavenly Father, who "makes his sun rise on the evil and on the good, and sends rain on the just and on the unjust" (*Mt* 5:45). And a shadow that follows his Son.

* * *

"Get up, take the child and his mother" (*Mt* 2:13), God told Saint Joseph.

The aim of this Apostolic Letter is to increase our love for this great saint, to encourage us to implore his intercession and to imitate his virtues and his zeal.

Indeed, the proper mission of the saints is not only to obtain miracles and graces, but to intercede for us before God, like Abraham[26] and Moses[27], and

---

[26] Cf. *Gen* 18:23-32.
[27] Cf. *Ex* 17:8-13; 32:30-35.

like Jesus, the "one mediator" (*1 Tim* 2:5), who is our "advocate" with the Father (*1 Jn* 2:1) and who "always lives to make intercession for [us]" (*Heb* 7:25; cf. *Rom* 8:34).

The saints help all the faithful "to strive for the holiness and the perfection of their particular state of life".[28] Their lives are concrete proof that it is possible to put the Gospel into practice.

Jesus told us: "Learn from me, for I am gentle and lowly in heart" (*Mt* 11:29). The lives of the saints too are examples to be imitated. Saint Paul explicitly says this: "Be imitators of me!" (*1 Cor* 4:16).[29] By his eloquent silence, Saint Joseph says the same.

Before the example of so many holy men and women, Saint Augustine asked himself: "What they could do, can you not also do?" And so he drew closer to his definitive conversion, when he could exclaim: "Late have I loved you, Beauty ever ancient, ever new!"[30]

We need only ask Saint Joseph for the grace of graces: our conversion.

---

[28] SECOND VATICAN ECUMENICAL COUNCIL, Dogmatic Constitution *Lumen Gentium*, 42.

[29] Cf. *1 Cor* 11:1; *Phil* 3:17; *1 Thess* 1:6.

[30] *Confessions*, VIII, 11, 27: PL 32, 761; X, 27, 38: PL 32, 795.

Let us now make our prayer to him:

Hail, Guardian of the Redeemer,
Spouse of the Blessed Virgin Mary.
To you God entrusted his only Son;
in you Mary placed her trust;
with you Christ became man.

Blessed Joseph, to us too,
show yourself a father
and guide us in the path of life.
Obtain for us grace, mercy and courage,
and defend us from every evil. Amen.

Given in Rome, at Saint John Lateran, on 8 December, Solemnity of the Immaculate Conception of the Blessed Virgin Mary, in the year 2020, the eighth of my Pontificate.

Franciscus

Year of Saint Joseph

Apostolic Penitentiary

DECREE

The gift of special Indulgences is granted on the occasion of the Year of Saint Joseph, announced by Pope Francis to celebrate the 150th anniversary of the proclamation of Saint Joseph as Patron of the Universal Church.

Today marks 150 years since the Decree *Quemadmodum Deus*, with which Bl. Pius IX, moved by the grave and sorrowful circumstances in which the Church was threatened by mankind's hostility, declared Saint Joseph the Patron of the Catholic Church.

In order to perpetuate the entrustment of the whole Church to the powerful patronage of the Guardian of Jesus, Pope Francis has established that, from today's date, the anniversary of the Decree of the proclamation as well as a day sacred to the Blessed Immaculate Virgin and Bride of Joseph most chaste, until 8 December 2021, a special Year of Saint Joseph will be celebrated, in which all faithful, after his example, may daily reinforce their own life of faith in complete fulfilment of God's will.

All the faithful will thus have the opportunity to commit themselves, with prayer and good works, to obtain, with the help of St Joseph, head of the heavenly Family of Nazareth, comfort and relief from the serious human and social tribulations that besiege the contemporary world today.

Devotion to the Guardian of the Redeemer has developed abundantly in the course of the history of the Church, which not only attributes to him among the loftiest worship, after that of his Bride, the Mother of God, but has also conferred many patronages upon him. The Magisterium of the Church continues to reveal great things, old and new, in this treasure that is Saint Joseph, like the householder of the Gospel of Matthew "who brings out of his treasure what is new and what is old" (*Mt* 13:52).

The gift of the Indulgences that the Apostolic Penitentiary kindly bestows during the Year of Saint Joseph, through this Decree issued according to Pope Francis' wish, will contribute greatly to the perfect accomplishment of the designated purpose.

The *Plenary Indulgence* is granted under the customary conditions (sacramental confession, Eucharistic communion and prayers according to the Holy Father's intentions) to the faithful who, with a soul detached from any sin, shall participate in the Year of Saint Joseph, in the occasions and with the modalities indicated by this Apostolic Penitentiary.

a. Saint Joseph, an authentic man of faith, invites us to rediscover our filial relationship with the Father, to renew our devotion to prayer, to dispose ourselves to listen and correspond with profound discernment to God's will. The *Plenary Indulgence* is granted to those who shall contemplate the Lord's Prayer for at least 30 minutes, or participate in a Spiritual Retreat of at least one day which involves a meditation on Saint Joseph.

b. The Gospel attributes to Saint Joseph the appellation "just man" (cf. *Mt* 1:19): he, guardian of the intimate secret that lies right at the bottom of the heart and soul",[1] depository of the mystery of God and therefore an ideal patron of the internal forum, spur us to rediscover the value of silence, prudence and integrity in carrying out our duties. The virtue of justice practiced by Saint Joseph in an exemplary manner is full adherence to divine law, which is the law of mercy, "for it is the very mercy of God that brings true justice to fulfilment".[2] There-

---

[1] Pius XI, *Address on the occasion of the proclamation of the heroic virtues of the Servant of God Emilia de Vialar*, in 'L'Osservatore Romano', year LXXV, 20-21 March 1935, 1.

[2] Francis, *General Audience* (3 February 2016).

fore those who, after the example of Saint Joseph, shall fulfil a work of corporal or spiritual work of mercy, will likewise be able to attain the gift of the *Plenary Indulgence*.

c. The primary aspect of Saint Joseph's vocation was that of being guardian of the Holy Family of Nazareth, spouse of the Blessed Virgin Mary and legal father of Jesus. In order that all Christian families may be inspired to recreate the same atmosphere of intimate communion, love and prayer that was lived by the Holy Family, the *Plenary Indulgence* is granted for the recitation of the Holy Rosary in families and among betrothed.

d. The Servant of God Pius XII, on 1 May 1955 instituted the Feast of Saint Joseph the Worker, "with the intent that the dignity of work be recognized by all, and that it inspires social life and laws, based on the fair distribution of rights and duties".[3] Therefore the *Plenary Indulgence* may be obtained by those who shall daily entrust their life to the protection of Saint Joseph, and all faithful who shall invoke through prayer the intercession of the Worker of Nazareth, so that those in search of work

[3] PIUS XII, *Address on the occasion of the Solemnity of Saint Joseph the Worker* (1 May 1955), in *Discorsi e Radiomessaggi di Sua Santità Pio XII*, XVII, 71-76.

may find employment and the work of all people may be more dignified.

e. The flight of the Holy Family to Egypt "shows us that God is there where man is in danger, where man suffers, where he runs away, where he experiences rejection and abandonment".[4] The *Plenary Indulgence* is granted to the faithful who shall recite the Litanies to Saint Joseph (for the Latin tradition), or the *Akathistos* to Saint Joseph, in their entirety or at least some part of it (for the Byzantine tradition), or some other prayer to Saint Joseph, proper to other liturgical traditions, in favour of the Church persecuted *ad intra* and *ad extra* and for the relief of all Christians who suffer any form of persecution.

Saint Teresa of Ávila recognized in Saint Joseph the protector for all the circumstances of life: "To other saints, the Lord seems to have given grace to help us in some of our necessities. But my experience is that Saint Joseph helps us in them all".[5] More recently, Saint John Paul II emphasized that the figure of Saint Joseph has ac-

---

[4] FRANCIS, *Angelus* (29 December 2013).

[5] TERESA D'ÁVILA, *Life*, VI, (translated from Italian, in EAD., *Tutte le opere*, ed. M. BETTETINI, Milan 2018, 67).

quired "a renewed relevance for the Church of our time, in relation to the new Christian millennium".[6]

To reaffirm the universality of Saint Joseph's patronage over the Church, in addition to the aforementioned occasions the Apostolic Penitentiary grants the *Plenary Indulgence* to the faithful who shall recite any prayer legitimately approved or act of piety in honour of Saint Joseph, for example, "To you, O Blessed Joseph", especially on the occasions of 19 March and 1 May, on the Feast of the Holy Family of Jesus, Mary and Joseph, on the Sunday of Saint Joseph (according to the Byzantine tradition), on the 19th of every month and every Wednesday, the day dedicated to the Saint's memory, according to the Latin tradition.

In the current context of the health emergency, the gift of the *Plenary Indulgence* extends particularly to the elderly, the sick, the suffering and all those who for legitimate reasons are unable to leave the house, and who with a soul detached from any sin and with the intention to fulfil, as soon as possible, the three customary conditions in their own home or wherever the impediment

[6] JOHN PAUL II, Apostolic Exhortation *Redemptoris Custos* on the figure and mission of Saint Joseph in the life of Christ and of the Church (15 August 1989), 32.

detains them, shall recite an act of piety in honour of Saint Joseph, Comfort of the Sick and Patron of a Happy Death, faithfully offering to God their suffering and the hardships of their life.

In order to pastorally facilitate the attainment of divine grace through the power of the Keys, this Penitentiary prays earnestly that all priests endowed with the appropriate faculties may offer themselves with a willing and generous soul to the celebration of the Sacrament of Penance and often administer Holy Communion to the infirm.

This Decree is valid for the Year of Saint Joseph, notwithstanding any disposition to the contrary.

Given in Rome, from the See of the Apostolic Penitentiary, on 8 December 2020

Cardinal MAURO PIACENZA

Major Penitentiary

KRZYSZTOF NYKIEL

Regent

L. + S.
Prot. n. 866/20/I

Saint Joseph and the Popes

While the biblical texts relating to Joseph, spouse of Mary and legal father of Jesus, are rather scarce, at first sight almost incomplete, there is an abundance of apocryphal literature on him, in particular the Protoevangelium of James. This is clearly due to the scarcity of information in the canonical books.

In the papal magisterium up to the end of the 19th century, only a few pronouncements on Saint Joseph are recorded, especially with regard to liturgical worship and the positioning of the saint's feast in the calendar of celebrations. This is the case of Pope Sixtus IV, who in 1479 included the feast of the Saint in his Breviary and in the Roman Missal on 19 March, and then Gregory XV, who in 1621 established that the feast of Saint Joseph was to be counted among the commanded feast days. It is only from Pius IX onwards that references to the Saint become more significant, and they remain so for almost all subsequent Popes, up to Francis, who began his Petrine ministry on the liturgical feast dedicated to Saint Joseph.

Pius IX (1846-1878)

From the beginning of his papacy he established the feast day and the liturgy for the patronage of Saint Joseph on the Third Sunday after Easter; he then strongly increased devotion to the Saint with a number of decrees. In particular, he pronounced on Joseph in six magisterial acts, of which certainly the best-remembered was the decree *Quemadmodum Deus*,[1] dated 8 December 1870, of the Sacred Congregation of Rites, by which he proclaimed the spouse of Mary the Patron of the Catholic Church.[2]

A very concise document, which represents the first important step of the pontifical magisterium on Saint Jo-

---

[1] *ASS* 6 (1870-1871), 193-194.

[2] The other five documents were: the Decree of the Sacred Congregation of Rites *Inclytus Patriarcha Joseph* (10 September 1847), which extends the feast of the patronage of Saint Joseph to all the Church; the Apostolic Letter *Iam Alias* (5 July 1861), which granted plenary indulgence for devotees of the perpetual worship of the Saint; the Decree *Cum In* (27 April 1865), which granted further indulgences for the worship of the Saint and the practice of the month of March; the Decree *Inclytum Patriarcham* (7 July 1871), which recognised the cult of Saint Joseph to be superior to that of the other saints; and finally the Decree *Iam Alias* (4 February 1877) of the Sacred Congregation of Indulgences and Sacred Relics, which approved and enriched the indulgences and prayer to the Saint, *Virginum custos*. See G. A. MATTANZA, *San Giuseppe, capo della Santa Famiglia, nel magistero pontificio da Pio IX ai nostri giorni. L'importanza di San Giuseppe per la figura del padre di famiglia*, Biblioteca Teologica 15, Eupress FTL – Ed. Cantagalli, Lugano – Siena 2019, 142-180: Don Giuseppe Attilio Mattanza's study, which has been extremely useful in this essay, and to which we refer for further study.

seph. It was published in the aftermath of a significant and tragic moment in the history of the Church and of Italy: the Sack of Rome, the suspension of Vatican Council I and the end of the temporal power of the papacy. Hence the Pontiff's decision to entrust the Universal Church to the protection of the Lord's putative father:

> Now, since in these very sad times the Church herself, attacked on all sides by enemies, is so oppressed by the gravest evils, [...] Our Most Holy Lord Pius IX, dismayed by this very recent and mournful state of affairs, entrusting himself and all the faithful to the most powerful patronage of the Holy Patriarch Joseph, [...] declared him Patron of the Catholic Church.[3]

With the Apostolic Letter *Patris Corde*, on the 150th anniversary of Pius IX's declaration, Pope Francis wishes "to share some personal reflections on this extraordinary figure, so close to our own human experience".[4]

Leo XIII (1878-1903)

As soon as he was elected Pope, in his homily to the cardinals in the conclave, he placed his pontificate

---

[3] *AAS* 6 (1870-1871), 193.

[4] POPE FRANCIS, Apostolic Letter *Patris Corde* (8 December 2020).

under the "most powerful" protection of Saint Joseph. And during his papacy, he wrote sixteen documents on the Saint.[5] Among these, the only one of its type among the texts dedicated by the Popes to the Spouse of Mary, is the encyclical *Quamquam Pluries* (15 August 1889), in which Pope Pecce presented all the doctrine on Saint Joseph and invoked him as the powerful protector against the adversities of the time. The encyclical concluded with the renowned prayer "To you, O blessed Joseph", to be recited at the end of the rosary during the month of October. "This custom", the Encyclical states, "should be repeated every year. To those who recite this prayer, We grant for each time an indulgence of seven years and seven Lents". This prayer asks for the Saint's patronage over the Church, the image of that bride, Mary, to whom the sacred bond binds him. The reason why he is the patron and protector of the Universal Church is that, just as Mary, the mother of the Lord, is the spiritual mother of all Christians, so Saint Joseph cares for all believers in Christ because they are entrusted to him according to the words of the prayer: "Defend, O most watchful

[5] Cf. MATTANZA, *San Giuseppe, capo della Santa Famiglia, nel magistero pontificio da Pio IX ai nostri giorni*. Cit., 191-231.

guardian of the Holy Family, the chosen off-spring of Jesus Christ".

The Pope also strongly promoted the practice of the 'month of March' in honour of the Saint. The encyclical is still the most important and, after John Paul II's *Redemptoris Custos*[6] (15 August 1989), the most comprehensive document published in honour of the putative father of Jesus.

Pius X (1903-1914)

Although he bore the name of Giuseppe, Joseph, Pius X did not distinguish himself by the publication of documents of particular relevance on Saint Joseph. On the other hand, through his magisterium he nurtured devotion to the Saint. In particular, with the Decree *Inclytum Patriarcham*[7] (18 March 1909), of the Sacred Congregation of Rites, he approved the litanies in honour of the Saint, authorizing their insertion in the liturgical books and enriching them with indulgences.[8] Before then the litanies of Saint Joseph that were known were primarily

[6] *AAS* 82 (1990), 5-34.

[7] *AAS* 3 (1909), 290.

[8] Another pronouncement to recall is that of 24 July 1911, with the Decree *De Diebus Festis*, in which Pius X established that the feast day of 19 March, falling within Lent, would be celebrated

47

those of the Carmelite Girolamo Graziano of the Mother of God, who composed them in 1597. They were then followed by various others. Pius X had the task of summarising them with the purpose of reordering the list of titles by which Saint Joseph could be invoked in public and private worship, entirely consistent with his predecessors Pius IX and Leo XIII.

Benedict XV (1914-1922)

He spoke on Saint Joseph in at least seven documents, with interventions related to liturgical and devotional aspects. The most important was the motu proprio *Bonum Sane*[9] (25 July 1920), for the 50th anniversary of the proclamation of Saint Joseph as Patron of the Universal Church, in which the Pontiff extolled his powerful and effective intercession against the evils and problems of the post-war period and indicated him as a model of virtue to be followed. Although the document is in continuity with the magisterium of his predecessors, it has a novelty that should be noted: the Pope further deepens the Josephine theology of the Church to the point of indicating – for the first time explicitly – the putative fa-

without octave, while on the Third Sunday after Easter the Feast would be solemnized with the octave.

[9] *AAS* 12 (1920), 313-317.

ther of Jesus as the special way to reach Christ, passing through the mediation of Mary:

> Through Joseph we go directly to Mary, and, through Mary, to the origin of all holiness, Jesus, who consecrated the domestic virtues by His obedience to Joseph and Mary. We therefore wish Christian families to be totally inspired by these wondrous examples of virtue, and to conform themselves to them. In this way, since the family is the fulcrum and the basis of human society, by strengthening domestic society with the presidium of holy purity, concord, and fidelity, a new vigour and, we would say, a new blood will circulate through the veins of human society, through the virtue of Christ; and there will follow not only an improvement in private customs, but also in the discipline of community and civil life.[10]

Pius XI (1922-1939)

In his magisterium we do not find a specific document, but there are at least fifteen addresses, two homilies and three encyclicals from which we can draw his teaching on the figure of Saint Joseph. There is a total of twenty brief pronouncements, almost all on the occasion

---

[10] BENEDICT XV, Motu proprio *Bonum Sane* (25 July 1920): *AAS* 12 (1920), 313.

of the feast day of 19 March.[11] From these we can see that St Joseph is, albeit in a different capacity from Mary, also a contributor to the mystery of the Incarnation and Redemption of the human race.

> Saint Joseph had the sole prerogative and the incomparable responsibility of being called by Divine Providence to guard a twofold treasure: a treasure of divinity in the person of Jesus Christ, a treasure of purity in the virginity of Mary Most Holy, a treasure, a divine secret, hitherto unknown to others, the secret of the Incarnation of the Word, of the life, of the passion, of the death of the Redeemer. This greatness of the role and responsibility of blessed Saint Joseph resides in his humility, his scrupulousness, his silence, passing in the midst of man and responding to what the Lord asked of him, in a truly wondrous and incomparable manner".[12]

Pius XII (1939-1958)

Pius XII did not dedicate a particular document to Saint Joseph. It is however possible to trace his magis-

[11] Refer to MATTANZA, *San Giuseppe, capo della Santa Famiglia, nel magistero pontificio da Pio IX ai nostri giorni.* Cit., 307-347.

[12] PIUS XI, *Address* to the Catholic men of Rome, 19 March 1929, in D. BERTETTO (ed.), *Discorsi di Pio XI*, Vol. 2., Libreria Editrice Vaticana, Vatican City 1985, 41-42.

terium throughout numerous addresses to married couples, on marriage, on the family and on the education of children. Among these, the most significant are the address of 29 June 1948 to the Italian Associations of Christian Workers, in which he indicated Saint Joseph as the patron of workers:

It was March 1945, when We greeted the representatives of the nascent Italian Associations of Christian Workers: a day of great, but also, almost, only of hope. Your Association took its first steps frankly and confidently; but the path was long and the goal far away. Today, as we contemplate your impressive following, we must recognise that the blessing of the Lord, which We invoked on your work, was powerful, and that the heavenly Patron, whom We gave to you at that time, Saint Joseph, faithful and righteous man, the quintessential worker, has prodigiously protected you".[13]

And the address pronounced on 1 May 1955, for the tenth year of the Italian Associations of Christian Workers, by which he instituted the liturgical feast of Saint Joseph the Worker:

[13] PIUS XII, *Address* to the many pilgrims belonging to the Italian Associations of Christian Workers (29 June 1948): *Atti e Discorsi di Pio XII,* X (1948), Pia Società San Paolo, Rome 1949, 164.

From the very beginning We placed your Associations under the powerful patronage of Saint Joseph. For there could be no better protector to help you imbue your lives with the spirit of the Gospel. As We said then, from the Heart of the Man-God, Saviour of the world, this spirit flows into you and into all men; but it is certain that no worker was ever so perfectly and deeply penetrated by it as the putative father of Jesus, who lived with Him in the closest intimacy and communion of family and work. So, if you wish to be close to Christ, we repeat to you today: "Ite ad Ioseph": Go to Joseph! (*Gen* 41:55). We love to announce to you Our determination to establish – as indeed we are establishing – the liturgical feast of Saint Joseph the Worker, assigning to it this very day, 1 May. Do you, dear workers, welcome this gift from Us? We are certain that you will, because the humble craftsman of Nazareth not only represents to God and Holy Church the dignity of the labourer, but He is also always the provident guardian of you and your families.[14]

John XXIII (1958-1963)

He was very devoted to the Saint whose name he was honoured to bear. Although he guided the Church for

[14] Pius XII, *Address* on the occasion of the Solemnity of Saint Joseph the Worker (1 May 1965), 406.

just under five years, his magisterium contains a substantial number of interventions on Saint Joseph. As many as eighty pronouncements, so numerous that they alone could constitute a treatise of theology on the Saint.[15] However, the good Pope's magisterium on Joseph was characterized above all by two important interventions: the inclusion of the name in the canon of the Mass and the proclamation of Saint Joseph as patron of the Second Vatican Ecumenical Council:

Everyone is interested in the Council, clerics and lay people, the great and the small from every part of the world, every social class, every race, every colour; and if a heavenly protector were to be designated to intercede from on high during its preparation and development, for that *virtus divina* (divine power) for which it seems destined to characterize an epoch in the history of the contemporary Church, there is no one in Heaven better that St. Joseph to whom to entrust this task, the head of the Family of Nazareth and protector of the Holy Church. [...] O Saint Joseph! Here, here is your place as *Protector Universalis Ecclesiae*. We have wished to offer you, through the voices and documents of our immediate predecessors of the last century – from

[15] Cf. MATTANZA, *San Giuseppe, capo della Santa Famiglia, nel magistero pontificio da Pio X ai nostri giorni.* Cit., 393-436.

Pius IX to Pius XII – a wreath of honour, echoing the testimonies of affectionate veneration which are now being raised from all Catholic nations and from all missionary regions. May you always be our protector. May your interior spirit of peace, silence, good work and prayer, at the service of the Holy Church, always enliven us and gladden us in union with your blessed Bride, our sweetest and Immaculate Mother, in the strongest and sweetest love of Jesus, the glorious and immortal King of the centuries and of peoples. So be it.[16]

Paul VI (1963-1978)

The magisterium of Giovanni Battista Montini on Saint Joseph is also characterized by numerous interventions,[17] especially in his various addresses, in which he not only emphasized the qualities of the Saint, but also brought out his mission in the Church. The importance and the greatness of the Saint for Paul VI are highlighted mainly within the mystery of the Incarnation of Christ, where he exercises his providential mission in the plan of the Redemption:

[16] JOHN XXIII, Apostolic Letter *Le voci* (19 March 1961): *AAS* 53 (1961), 205.

[17] Cf MATTANZA, *San Giuseppe, capo della Santa Famiglia, nel magistero pontificio da Pio IX ai nostri giorni.* Cit., 437-484.

We are celebrating the feast of St Joseph, Patron of the Universal Church. It is a feast which interrupts the austere and passionate meditation of Lent, which is entirely absorbed in the penetration of the mystery of Redemption and in the application of the spiritual discipline which the celebration of such a mystery brings with it. It is a feast which calls our attention to another mystery of the Lord, the Incarnation, and invites us to think back to it in the poor, gentle, most human scene, the Gospel scene of the Holy Family of Nazareth, in which this other mystery was historically fulfilled. The Blessed Virgin appears to us in this most humble of Gospel pictures; next to her is Saint Joseph, and between them, Jesus. Our eyes and our devotion today turn to Saint Joseph, the silent, hard-working blacksmith, who gave Jesus not his birth, but his civil status, his social category, his economic status, his professional experience, his family background and his human education. This relationship between Saint Joseph and Jesus should be observed carefully, because it can help us to understand many things about the plan of God, who came into this world to live as a man among men, but at the same time as their teacher and saviour.[18]

[18] PAUL VI, *Homily* on the occasion of the Fiat pilgrimage (19 March 1964): *Insegnamenti di Paolo VI,* II (1964), 186.

For Paul VI the figure of Saint Joseph is also profoundly rooted in the virtue of humility, and such a virtue is to be imitated in every area of Christian life, in the Church as in the family, and by individual Christians from every social category:

Saint Joseph presents himself to us in the most unexpected guises. We might have supposed him to be a powerful man, opening the way for the Christ who had come into the world; or perhaps a prophet, a sage, a man of priestly activity, in order to welcome the Son of God who had entered the human race and our conversation. Instead, he is the most ordinary, modest, humble person imaginable. [...] Could we then ignore this figure, not dwell on him? No, not at all: for then we would not understand the doctrine taught by the Divine Master: the Good News from its first characteristic form, that of being announced to the poor, to the humble, to those who need to be consoled and redeemed. That is why the Gospel of the Beatitudes begins with this introducer, named Joseph. [...] Let us also, with filial devotion, like people of the house, approach the door of the humble workshop of Nazareth and each of us pray to Joseph: give me a hand, a support; protect me too. There is no life that is not beset by many dangers, by temptations, weaknesses and failings. Joseph, silent and good, faithful, meek, strong and unconquered, teaches us what we must do; and he certainly provides help with exquisite goodness.[19]

But it is above all his participation in the mystery of the Redemption that Paul VI places at the basis of devotion to Saint Joseph:

This is the secret of Saint Joseph's greatness, which is consistent with his humility: having made his life a service, a sacrifice, to the mystery of the Incarnation and to the redemptive mission that is linked to it; having used the legal authority that belonged to him over the sacred family to make a total gift of himself, his life, his work; converting his human vocation to domestic love in the superhuman oblation of himself, his heart and all his abilities, in the love placed at the service of the Messiah who grew in his home, his nominal son and son of David, but in reality the son of Mary and son of God.[20]

[19] PAUL VI, *Homily* at the Mass for the Feast of Saint Joseph (19 March 1968): *Insegnamenti di Paolo VI,* VI (1968), 1154.

[20] PAUL VI, *Homily* for the Feast of Saint Joseph, on the occasion of the Episcopal Consecration of four prelates of the Curia (19 March 1966): *Insegnamenti di Paolo VI,* IV (1966), 111.

John Paul II (1978-2005)

He is the Pontiff who to date has produced the richest and most extensive magisterium on Saint Joseph. Depending on the circumstances, he has dealt more or less extensively with the putative father of Jesus, sometimes devoting entire specific documents or parts of them, at other times simply quoting him indirectly. Giuseppe Mattanza[21] recorded his magisterial interventions as follows: 340 speeches, 196 homilies, 105 *Angelus* or *Regina Caeli*, 33 greetings, 33 messages, 32 apostolic letters, 20 decrees, 16 letters, 11 apostolic constitutions, 8 apostolic exhortations, 5 encyclicals, 3 allocutions, 3 prayers, 2 acts of entrustment, 2 letters decrees, one Directory for Popular Piety and the Liturgy, one radio message, one meditation, one preface, one thanksgiving, and one telegram, a total of 815 interventions. Such a large amount of documents is not only the result of his long pontificate of 27 years, but also of John Paul II's deep personal devotion to Saint Joseph, held since his youth.

In his autobiography, the Polish Pope says that for him:

[21] Cf MATTANZA, *San Giuseppe, capo della Santa Famiglia, nel magistero pontificio da Pio IX ai nostri giorni.* Cit., 498-499.

Devotion to Saint Joseph is another thing I would associate with my life in Kraków. The Bernardine Sisters on Poselska Street, near the episcopal palace, have a church dedicated to Saint Joseph, where they have perpetual adoration of the Blessed Sacrament. In my free time, I would go there to pray, and often my eyes would be drawn toward a beautiful image of Our Lord's foster father, an image greatly venerated in that church, where I once conducted a retreat for attorneys. I have always liked to think of Saint Joseph in the setting of the Holy Family: Jesus, Mary, and Joseph. I used to pray to all three of them for help with various problems. I can well understand the unity and love that characterized the Holy Family: three hearts, one love. I entrusted the Family Apostolate to Saint Joseph's particular care. In Kraków, at Podgórze, there is another church dedicated to Saint Joseph. I often went there during pastoral visitations.[22]

And how can one forget the gesture John Paul II made in giving his papal ring to the painting of Saint Joseph, conserved in the Carmelite convent in Wadowice,

[22] JOHN PAUL II, *Rise, let us be on our way*, Mondadori, Milan 2004, 106-107.

his place of birth. It was on the occasion of the twenty-fifth anniversary of his pontificate, 16 October 2003.

In the extensive Josephine magisterium of Wojtyła, the central place is occupied by the Apostolic Exhortation *Redemptoris Custos* of 15 August 1989. It was published on the occasion of the centenary of the Leo XIII's encyclical *Quamquam Pluries*, and completes the trilogy initiated with the encyclical *Redemptor hominis* (1979) on the figure of Jesus Christ the Redeemer, followed by the encyclical *Redemptoris Mater* (1987), on Mary Mother of the Redeemer, concluded with the exhortation on the Guardian of the Redeemer. As already mentioned, the exhortation is currently the most extensive and complete document of the pontifical magisterium on Saint Joseph, who is indicated as a concrete example for everyone to imitate in their own lifestyle:

> May Saint Joseph become for all of us an exceptional teacher in the service of Christ's saving mission, a mission which is the responsibility of each and every member of the Church: husbands and wives, parents, those who live by the work of their hands or by any other kind of work, those called to the contemplative life or those called to the apostolate.
> This just man, who bore within himself the entire heritage of the Old Covenant, was also brought into the

"beginning" of the New and Eternal Covenant in Jesus Christ. May he show us the paths of this saving Covenant as we stand at the threshold of the next millennium, in which there must be a continuation and further development of the "fullness of time" that belongs to the ineffable mystery of the incarnation of the Word. May Joseph obtain for the Church and for the world, as well as for each of us, the blessing of the Father, Son and Holy Spirit.[23]

Benedict XVI (2005-2013)

Baptised Joseph, he often referred to the figure of the Holy Patriarch in his teachings, inviting believers on many occasions to follow the school of Saint Joseph, to imitate his virtues, and to devote themselves to him in prayer. Mattanza records 205 interventions of the Pope emeritus on the Saint, divided as follows: 80 speeches, 42 *Angelus* or *Regina Caeli*, 39 homilies, 12 messages, 11 letters, 12 decrees, 4 apostolic letters, 2 decretal letters, one Apostolic Exhortation, one Apostolic Constitution, one greeting.[24]

[23] JOHN PAUL II, Apostolic Exhortation *Redemptoris Custos* (15 August 1989), 32: *AAS* 82 (1990), 34.
[24] Cf MATTANZA, *San Giuseppe, capo della Santa Famiglia, nel magistero pontificio da Pio IX ai nostri giorni.* Cit., 546-547.

Pope Ratzinger's interventions are not only magisterial interventions, but pages of genuinely personal confidences, of rare beauty, of a Christian devoted to the putative father of Jesus, such as when he indicates Saint Joseph as the confidant of his own prayer:

> Dear friends, in a few days' time, we will be celebrating the solemnity of Saint Joseph, Patron of Workers. ... For my part I, who bear his name, am pleased today to be able to point him out to you not only as a heavenly Protector and Intercessor for every worthwhile initiative, but first and foremost as one to whom you can confide your prayer and your ordinary commitment, which are surely marked both by satisfactions and disappointments in your daily life and, I would say, tenacious search for God's justice in human affairs. Saint Joseph himself will help you put into practice Jesus' demanding exhortation: "Seek first the Kingdom of God and His righteousness" (cf. *Mt* 6: 33).[25]

And then when he suggests imitating the Saint's quality of silence, full of faith, that guides his every thought and action:

[25] BENEDICT XVI, *Address* to Italian Christian Executives (UCID) (4 March 2006): *Insegnamenti di Benedetto XVI,* II, 1 (2006), 286.

Saint Joseph's silence does not express an inner emptiness but, on the contrary, the fullness of the faith he bears in his heart and which guides his every thought and action. It is a silence thanks to which Joseph, in unison with Mary, watches over the Word of God, known through the Sacred Scriptures, continuously comparing it with the events of the life of Jesus; a silence woven of constant prayer, a prayer of blessing of the Lord, of the adoration of his holy will and of unreserved entrustment to his providence. It is no exaggeration to think that it was precisely from his "father" Joseph that Jesus learned – at the human level – that steadfast interiority which is a presupposition of authentic justice, the "superior justice" which he was one day to teach his disciples (cf. *Mt* 5: 20).

Let us allow ourselves to be "filled" with Saint Joseph's silence! In a world that is often too noisy, that encourages neither recollection nor listening to God's voice, we are in such deep need of it. During this season of preparation for Christmas, let us cultivate inner recollection in order to welcome and cherish Jesus in our own lives.[26]

---

[26] BENEDICT XVI, *Angelus* (18 December 2005): *Insegnamenti di Benedetto XVI*, I (2005), 787.

Finally, the docility of Saint Joseph, in placing himself in obedience to the Word of God:

Saint Joseph, my personal Patron and the Patron of the Holy Church: a humble saint, a humble worker who was made worthy to be the Custodian of the Redeemer. Saint Matthew describes Saint Joseph with one word: he was a "just" man, "*dikaios*", from "*dike*", and in the vision of the Old Testament, as we find it, for example, in Psalm 1: the man who is immersed in the word of God, who lives in the word of God and does not experience the Law as a "*yoke*" but rather as a "*joy*", who dwells in – we might say – the Law as a "Gospel". Saint Joseph was just, he was immersed in the word of God, written and transmitted through the wisdom of his people, and he was trained and called in this very way to know the Incarnate Word – the Word who came among us as a man – and was predestined to look after, to protect this Incarnate Word; this remained his mission for ever: to look after Holy Church and Our Lord. Let us entrust ourselves at this moment to his care, let us pray that he may help us in our humble service. Let us go ahead courageously under this protection. We are grateful for the humble saints, and let us pray the Lord to make us too humble in our service and thereby holy in the company of the saints.[27]

Pope Francis (2013-)

Pope Bergoglio has always been a devotee of Saint Joseph. In particular, he has always kept the statue of the sleeping Saint Joseph, a popular icon in Latin America, in the rooms where he has lived and worked. Even now, the Pontiff has this image of the saint in his study at the Casa Santa Marta, and his devotion to what it represents enjoyed sudden worldwide popularity when the Pope spoke about it a few years ago at the *World Meeting of Families* in Manila:

> I have great love for Saint Joseph, because he is a man of silence and strength. On my table I have an image of Saint Joseph sleeping. Even when he is asleep, he is taking care of the Church! Yes! We know that he can do that. So when I have a problem, a difficulty, I write a little note and I put it underneath Saint Joseph, so that he can dream about it! In other words I tell him: pray for this problem! Next, rising with Jesus and

[27] BENEDICT XVI, *Conclusion of the spiritual exercises of the Roman Curia* (19 March 2011): *Insegnamenti di Benedetto XVI,* VII, 1 (2011), 343.

Mary. Those precious moments of repose, of resting with the Lord in prayer, are moments we might wish to prolong. But like Saint Joseph, once we have heard God's voice, we must rise from our slumber; we must get up and act (cf. *Rom* 13:11). In our families, we have to get up and act! Faith does not remove us from the world, but draws us more deeply into it.[28]

Going back in time, Francis celebrated the Mass of the beginning of his pontificate in 2013 on the day the Church commemorates the Saint, an occasion chosen and desired by the Argentine Pope because he has always seen the strength and wisdom of God in the Spouse of the Virgin Mary. On that occasion, he explained in his homily that:

> Joseph is a "protector" because he is able to hear God's voice and be guided by his will; and for this reason he is all the more sensitive to the persons entrusted to his safekeeping. He can look at things realistically, he is in touch with his surroundings, he can make truly wise decisions. In him, dear friends, we learn how to respond to God's call, readily and willingly.[29]

[28] FRANCIS, *Address to families*, Mall of Asia Arena, Manila (16 January 2015).

[29] FRANCIS, *Homily* of the Mass for the beginning of the Petrine Ministry of the Bishop of Rome (19 March 2013).

On 1 May 2013, among the first acts of his Pontificate, Pope Francis confirmed Pope Benedict's desire and decreed that the name of St. Joseph, the Spouse of the Blessed Virgin Mary, be added in Eucharistic Prayers II, III and IV.

But it is in the chapel of his residence, Santa Marta, that the Pope has long reflected on this Saint to whom he confides every concern. During Mass on 18 December 2017, he suggested that we turn to Mary's Spouse when "we don't understand things, when we have a lot of problems, a lot of anxiety, darkness". And he even proposed a prayer to recite:

This is the great Joseph whom God needed to carry forward the mystery of leading his people back toward the new creation. This specific example teaches us many things on which to reflect, but above all it can give us the courage to go to him when we do not understand things, when we have a lot of problems, a lot of anxiety, darkness and simply say to him: "Help us, you who know how to walk in the dark, you who know how to listen to God's voice, you who know how to move ahead in silence".[30]

[30] FRANCIS, *Homily* at morning Mass, Casa Santa Marta (18 December 2017).

And in another morning Mass, Pope Francis under-
lined that Joseph is the man who acts even as he slept
because he dreamed about what God wanted:

> Today I would like to ask, may he give us all the capacity
> to dream, because when we dream of great things, of
> beautiful things, we approach God's dream, the things
> that God dreams of for us. May he give young peo-
> ple – because he was young – the capacity to dream, to
> risk and take on the difficult tasks that they saw in their
> dreams. And may he give us all the fidelity that generally
> grows in a just attitude, he was just, it grows in silence –
> few words – and it grows in the tenderness that is able
> to safeguard our own weaknesses and those of others.[31]

On the 150th anniversary of Pius IX's declaration
of Saint Joseph as Patron Saint of the Catholic Church
on 8 December 1870, Pope Francis once again places the
Church and all of humanity under the Saint's protection.
Today, as then, the community of believers is facing a serious historical moment. Today, the enemy is an invisible
being that spreads pandemics, suffering and in many cases death. The Pontiff notes, however, that despite this,
many ordinary people are doing their best, in silence and

[31] FRANCIS, *Homily* at morning Mass, Casa Santa Marta (20
March 2017).

without ostentation, to provide charitable service to their brothers and sisters in need, following the example of Saint Joseph. And he explains that the desire to write the Apostolic Letter *Patris Corde*:

> increased during these months of pandemic, when we experienced, amid the crisis, how "our lives are woven together and sustained by ordinary people, people often overlooked. People who do not appear in newspaper and magazine headlines, or on the latest television show, yet in these very days are surely shaping the decisive events of our history. Doctors, nurses, storekeepers and supermarket workers, cleaning personnel, caregivers, transport workers, men and women working to provide essential services and public safety, volunteers, priests, men and women religious, and so very many others. They understood that no one is saved alone… How many people daily exercise patience and offer hope, taking care to spread not panic, but shared responsibility. How many fathers, mothers, grandparents and teachers are showing our children, in small everyday ways, how to accept and deal with a crisis by adjusting their routines, looking ahead and encouraging the practice of prayer. How many are praying, making sacrifices and interceding for the good of all".[32] Each

---

[32] FRANCIS, *Meditation in the Time of Pandemic* (27 March 2020): *L'Osservatore Romano*, 29 March 2020, 10.

of us can discover in Joseph – the man who goes unnoticed, a daily, discreet and hidden presence – an intercessor, a support and a guide in times of trouble. Saint Joseph reminds us that those who appear hidden or in the shadows can play an incomparable role in the history of salvation. A word of recognition and of gratitude is due to them all.[33]

Pope Francis writes: "The aim of this Apostolic Letter is to increase our love for this great saint, to encourage us to implore his intercession and to imitate his virtues and his zeal".[34] And to continue entrusting the Church to its Patron, the Pope has established that from 8 December 2020, "the anniversary of the Decree of the proclamation as well as a day sacred to the Blessed Immaculate Virgin and Bride of Joseph most chaste, until 8 December 2021, a special Year of Saint Joseph will be celebrated, in which all faithful, after his example, may daily reinforce their own life of faith in complete fulfilment of God's will".[35]

"All the faithful will thus have the opportunity to commit themselves, with prayer and good works, to obtain, with the help of St Joseph, head of the heavenly

[33] FRANCIS, Apostolic Letter *Patris Corde* (8 December 2020).

[34] *Ivi.*

[35] APOSTOLIC PENITENTIARY, *Decree granting the gift of special Indulgences on the occasion of the Year of Saint Joseph* (8 December 2020).

Family of Nazareth, comfort and relief from the serious human and social tribulations that besiege the contemporary world today".[36]

The faithful, participating in the Year of Saint Joseph "with a soul detached from any sin", can obtain a Plenary Indulgence under the customary conditions (sacramental confession, Eucharistic communion and prayer according to the intentions of the Holy Father), through the various ways the Pentintiary listed in the Decree that accompanied the Apostolic Letter *Patris Corde*.

[36] *Ivi.*

Prayers to Saint Joseph

Virginum custos

O guardian and father of virgins,
Saint Joseph to whose faithful guardianship
was entrusted innocence itself, Christ Jesus,
and the Virgin of virgins, Mary,
I beseech thee and entreat thee
for these thy dear treasures, Jesus and Mary,
that, preserved from all uncleanliness,
pure in mind and heart, and chaste in body,
that I may always serve
serve Jesus and Mary most purely.
So be it.

Blessed Pius IX

To you, O Blessed Joseph

To you, O Blessed Joseph,
in tribulation we turn to thee
and confidently invoke your patronage
after that of thy most holy Bride.
O Blessed Joseph, through that sacred bond of charity
that binds you to the Immaculate Virgin Mother of God,
and for the paternal love you bore to the infant Jesus,
We humbly beg you to look graciously
upon the dear legacy Jesus Christ
obtained with His Blood,
and by your power and help, provide for our needs.
Protect, O most watchful Guardian of the divine Family,
the chosen children of Jesus Christ;
Keep from us, O most loving Father,
All blight of error and corruption;
Aid us from on high in this struggle
against the power of darkness,
our most valiant protector;
and just as you once saved the infant Jesus
from mortal danger,
so now defend God's holy Church
from the snares of the enemy and from all adversity:
Shield us by your constant protection, so that,

supported by your example
and strengthened by your help,
we may live virtuously, die piously,
and obtain eternal bliss in heaven.
Amen.

Leo XIII

Litanies to Saint Joseph

Lord, have mercy.	*Lord, have mercy.*
Christ, have mercy.	*Christ, have mercy.*
Lord, have mercy.	*Lord, have mercy.*
Christ, hear us.	*Christ, hear us.*
Christ, graciously hear us.	*Christ, graciously hear us.*
God, the Father of Heaven.	*Have mercy on us.*
God the Son, Redeemer of the world.	*Have mercy on us.*
God the Holy Spirit.	*Have mercy on us.*
Holy Trinity, One God.	*Have mercy on us.*

Holy Mary, *(R.)*	*Pray for us.*
Saint Joseph, *R.*	
Renowned offspring of David, *R.*	
Light of Patriarchs, *R.*	
Spouse of the Mother of God, *R.*	
Chaste guardian of the Virgin, *R.*	
Caring father of the Son of God, *R.*	
Diligent protector of Christ, *R.*	
Head of the Holy Family, *R.*	
Joseph most just, *R.*	
Joseph most chaste, *R.*	
Joseph most prudent, *R.*	
Joseph most strong, *R.*	
Joseph most obedient, *R.*	
Joseph most faithful, *R.*	

Mirror of patience, *R.*
Lover of poverty, *R.*
Model of artisans, *R.*
Glory of home life, *R.*
Guardian of virgins, *R.*
Pillar of families, *R.*
Solace of the wretched, *R.*
Hope of the sick, *R.*
Patron of the dying, *R.*
Terror of demons, *R.*
Protector of Holy Church, *R.*

Lamb of God, who takes away
    the sins of the world.   *Spare us, O Lord!*
Lamb of God, who takes away
    the sins of the world.   *Graciously hear us, O Lord!*
Lamb of God, who takes away
    the sins of the world.   *Have mercy on us.*

V. He made him the lord of his household.
R. *And prince over all his possessions.*

Let us pray.

O God, in your ineffable providence you were pleased
to choose Blessed Joseph to be the spouse of your most

holy Mother; grant, we beg you, that we may be worthy to have him for our intercessor in heaven whom on earth we venerate as our Protector. You who live and reign forever and ever. Amen.

Saint Pius X

Saint Joseph the craftsman

O glorious Patriarch Saint Joseph,
humble and righteous craftsman of Nazareth,
who gave to all Christians, but especially to us
the example of a perfect life
in diligent work and admirable union with Mary and Jesus,
assist us in our daily toil
so that we too
can find in it the effective means of glorifying the Lord,
to sanctify ourselves and to be useful to the society
in which we live,
the supreme ideals of all our actions.
Obtain for us from the Lord
O our beloved Protector,
humility and simplicity of heart,
affection for work and benevolence
Toward those who are our companions in it,
conformity to the divine will
in the inevitable travails of this life
and joy in bearing them,
awareness of our specific social mission
and sense of our responsibility,
spirit of discipline and prayer...
Accompany us in prosperous times

when everything invites us to taste honestly
the fruits of our labours;
but sustain us in the hours of sadness,
when the sky seems to close in on us
and even the tools of our work
seem to rebel in our hands.
Grant that, in imitation of you
we keep our eyes fixed on our Mother Mary,
your most sweet Bride,
who in a corner of your modest workshop silently spun,
with the sweetest smile on her lips;
and let us not turn our eyes away from Jesus
who laboured with thee at thy carpenter's bench;
that we may lead on earth
a peaceful and holy life,
a prelude to that eternally happy life
that awaits us in Heaven,
for ever and ever.
Amen.

Pius XII

O Saint Joseph, chosen by God

O Saint Joseph
chosen by God to be on this earth
the Custodian of Jesus and most pure Spouse of Mary,
You have spent your life
in the perfect fulfilment of duty,
supporting with the work of your hands
the Holy Family of Nazareth,
protect us in your favour who
confidently turn to Thee.
You know our aspirations,
our anxieties, our hopes:
to You we turn,
because we know that in You we can find the one who
protects us.
You too have experienced
trial, fatigue, weariness;
but your soul, filled with the deepest peace,
rejoiced in the intimacy
with the Son of God entrusted to you,
and with Mary, his sweetest Mother.
Help us to understand
that we are not alone in our work,
to be able to discover Jesus beside us,

to welcome Him with grace
and keep Him with fidelity
as you have done.
Obtain that in our family
all may be sanctified
in charity, patience, justice and the pursuit of good.
Amen.

Saint John XXIII

O, Saint Joseph, Custodian of Jesus

O, Saint Joseph, Custodian of Jesus,
Most Chaste Spouse of Mary
who spent your life in perfect fulfilment of duty,
supporting with the work of your hands
the Holy Family of Nazareth,
protect with favour those who, trustfully, turn to Thee.
You know their aspirations,
their anxieties and their hopes:
and they turn to Thee, because they know that in Thee
they will find one who understands and protects them.
You too have experienced trial, fatigue, weariness:
but even in the midst of the cares of material life,
your soul, filled with the deepest peace,
rejoiced with unfathomable joy at the intimacy
with the Son of God,
entrusted to you, and with Mary, his sweetest Mother.
Let your protégés also understand
that they are not alone in their work,
but are able to discover Jesus beside them,
welcome Him with grace, keep him faithfully,
as you have done.
And obtain that in every family, in every workshop,
in every laboratory,
wherever a Christian works, all may be sanctified in charity,

in patience, in justice, in the pursuit of good works,
so that the gifts of heavenly predilection
may descend in abundance.
Amen.

Saint John XXIII

Saint Joseph, Patron of the Church

O Saint Joseph, Patron of the Church,
Thou who, alongside the Incarnate Word
worked every day to earn your bread
drawing from Him the strength to live and to toil;
Thou who hast experienced the anxiety of tomorrow,
the bitterness of poverty, the precariousness of work;
You who today radiate the example of your person,
humble before men
but very great before God;
look upon the immense family entrusted to you!
Bless the Church
urging her ever more along the paths
of evangelical fidelity,
and keep peace in the world,
that peace which alone can guarantee the development
of peoples
and the complete fulfilment of human hopes:
for the good of humanity
for the mission of the Church
for the glory of the Most Holy Trinity.
Amen.

Saint Paul VI

Saint Joseph, with you, through you

Saint Joseph, with you, through you,
we bless the Lord!
He chose you among all men
to be the chaste Spouse of Mary,
the one who would remain at the threshold
of the mystery
of her divine Maternity
and who, after her
would accept it in faith
as the work of the Holy Spirit.
You gave Jesus legal paternity
in the lineage of David.
You constantly watched over
the Mother and the Child with an affectionate concern,
to enable them to accomplish their mission.
The Saviour Jesus deigned to submit himself
to You as to a father
throughout his childhood and adolescence,
and receive from You the teachings for human life,
while You shared his life
in adoration of its mystery.
Continue to protect the whole Church,
the family born of the salvation brought by Jesus!

See the spiritual and material needs
of all those who beg your intercession:
through you they are sure to find Mary's maternal gaze
and the hand of Jesus to assist them.
Amen.

Saint John Paul II

O *dear Saint Joseph*

O dear Saint Joseph
friend and protector of all,
Guardian of Jesus and of all those who invoke your help,
you are great because you obtain from God
all that men ask of you.
Please receive my prayer:
watch over and protect all families
so that they may live the harmony, unity, faith and love
that reigned in the Family of Nazareth.
Look with particular tenderness at the families
of the unemployed,
give them all work,
so that by their labour they may create a better world
and give praise to God the Creator.
I entrust the Church to you
in particular the Pope, the Bishops, the priests, and all the
missionaries
that they may feel sustained by your paternity.
Who can love them more than you, dear Saint Joseph?
Protect all consecrated persons
that they may find in your obedience
and adherence to the will of God
the example of living in silence,

humility and missionary spirit
the life of union with God
that makes them happy in the fulfilment
of the divine Will.
The joy of feeling they belong to God is so great
that it has no comparison;
only in God is all happiness found.
Saint Joseph, hear my prayer!
Amen.

Saint John Paul II

Act of entrustment to the intercession of Saint Joseph

Protect, O Holy Guardian, this our nation.

Enlighten those responsible for the common good, so that they might know – like you do – how to care for those entrusted to their responsibility.

Grant intelligence of knowledge to those seeking adequate means for the health and physical well-being of their brothers and sisters.

Sustain those who are spending themselves for those in need, even at the cost of their own safety: volunteers, nurses, doctors who are on the front lines in curing the sick.

Bless, St Joseph, the Church: beginning with her ministers, make her the sign and instrument of your light and your goodness.

Accompany, O St Joseph, our families: with your prayerful silence, create harmony between parents and their children, in a special way with the youngest.

Preserve the elderly from loneliness: grant that no one might be left in desperation from abandonment and discouragement.

Comfort those who are the most frail, encourage those who falter, intercede for the poor.

With the Virgin Mother, beg the Lord to liberate the world from every form of pandemic.

Amen.

Pope Francis

Guardian of the Redeemer

Hail, Guardian of the Redeemer,
Spouse of the Blessed Virgin Mary.
To you God entrusted his only Son;
in you Mary placed her trust;
with you Christ became man.
Blessed Joseph, to us too,
show yourself a father
and guide us in the path of life.
Obtain for us grace, mercy and courage,
and defend us from every evil.
Amen.

Pope Francis

Glorious Patriarch

Glorious Patriarch Saint Joseph,
whose power makes the impossible possible,
come to my aid in these times of anguish and difficulty.
Take under your protection the serious and troubling
situations that I commend to you,
that they may have a happy outcome.
My beloved father, all my trust is in you.
Let it not be said that I invoked you in vain,
and since you can do everything with Jesus and Mary,
show me that your goodness is as great as your power.
Amen.

Recited by Pope Francis every morning

Consecration to Saint Joseph

Saint Joseph, I consecrate myself to you
to be forever your imitator,
your lovable son.
Take possession of me,
do of my body and my soul
what you would do
of your body and your soul,
for the glory of Jesus.
He also entrusted himself to you
so fully that he allowed himself to be taken
where you thought it was appropriate,
from establish yourself for his father
and obey you as the most docile son.
Sacred Heart of Jesus,
thank you for giving us Joseph for father
and for giving us everything you have
and everything you are.
Let me give you back love for love;
I ask you through intercession
and in the name of Saint Joseph!

Blessed Charles de Foucauld

Glorious Saint Joseph

Glorious Saint Joseph,
whose power extends to all our necessities
and can render possible for us the most impossible things,
open thy fatherly eyes to the needs of thy children.
In the trouble and distress which afflict us,
we confidently have recourse to thee!
Deign to take under your charitable charge
this important and difficult matter,
cause of our worries.
Amen.

Saint Francis de Sales

Your name, O Joseph, is the consolation of mortals

Draw us to you, most loving Joseph: we will follow you!
Angels of Heaven, Saints of Heaven,
you who rejoice when the loving name of Joseph
resounds in the Holy City,
teach us the esteem in which we must hold him
and the respect with which we must pronounce it!
Thy name, O Joseph, delight of Heaven,
is the honour of Earth, is the consolation of mortals:
It invigorates the weary, it comforts the afflicted,
it heals the sick,
softens hardened hearts,
helps in temptations, frees from the wiles of the devil,
obtains all manner of good things for those
who invoke him
and shares in the power of the holy names
of Jesus and Mary.
May such a beautiful name be written with the characters
of stars in the vaults of the firmament,
that it may be seen and spoken by all the world!
May it be carved by our love, so that all men
may love and honour it!
May it be in my mouth and in my heart!
Amen.

Blessed Bartolo Longo

Praise to Saint Joseph

If the glory of the Saints in Heaven
is proportionate to their merits
and the graces received on earth;
if Jesus Christ promises an eternal reward
to whoever gives a poor man
a glass of water in His name;
to what degree of glory
were you raised up with God, O Joseph,
Who were enriched with so many graces
and of perfection incomprehensible to the human mind?
What reward should you not receive
from the most free hand of God,
You who gave so much care to Jesus Christ,
not as we do, in the person of the poor
but in His own person
and in that of His Divine Mother?
What must not be the greatness of your power in Heaven,
after you guided the Son of God on earth
and saw him for thirty years subjected to your bidding?
Yes, O my most glorious Protector,
I confess this in the sight of Heaven and Earth,
You occupy a very high place with Jesus and Mary.
All Paradise magnifies your glory

and pays homage to the august qualities
that raise thee above all the angelic hosts.
Let us, from this vale of tears,
lift up our gaze to the sublime throne where you are seated,
and unite our voices to the concert of the blessed spirits
to exalt your greatness
honour your virtues and implore
your mighty protection.
And confirm in our hearts
faith, hope and charity
that, having loved and faithfully served you in this life
we can continue for all eternity to bless you
with Jesus and Mary in Heaven.
Amen.

Blessed Bartolo Longo

Prostrate at your feet

Prostrate at your feet, O great saint,
I venerate you as the Father of my Lord and my God.
You are the Head of the Holy Family,
and a cause of joy and delight to the Holy Trinity.
What a glory for you to be the Father of a Son
who is the Only Begotten of God!
What a blessing to know that you are a father to us
and that we are your children.
Yes, we are your children
because we are brothers and sisters of Jesus Christ,
who wanted to be called your Son.
As your children,
we have a right to the tenderness of your paternal heart.
This tenderness and this goodness
We implore, in your name, of the adorable Jesus
So dear and sweet to your Heart.
Accept us therefore!
Take us under your protection!
Teach us to love holy poverty, patience, prudence,
kindness, modesty, and purity.
Be our refuge and solace in all our pains,
in all our needs,
in our lifetime and at the hour of our death.
Amen.

Blessed Bartolo Longo

O great Saint Joseph

O great Saint Joseph
who was chosen by God for the most sublime mystery
that can be entrusted to a pure creature,
You are the angel of purity, the chosen lily of virginity,
For which God himself was pleased to call you
the Father of his Only-Begotten,
and transmitted to Thee his rights.
He who created all the hearts of men,
placed in you a Father's Heart
and at the same time gave to Jesus, through you,
the heart of a Son.
O most blessed Joseph, may you be my Father too!
Be a Father to all those whom Jesus loved to the point
of becoming their brother!
I prostrate myself at your feet with all the affection
of my soul,
beseeching you to accept the offering of my heart,
that you may make it pure
and thus present it to Jesus, your Son,
to whom I consecrate it forever and without reserve.
Pray to Him to remove sin
from this most miserable heart,
the love of pleasure and everything

that does not please Him;
to inflame it with the sacred fire of his holy love,
to adorn it with all the virtues
of which his adorable Heart has given us
such admirable examples
so that, taking full possession of it as of now,
may he reign over it for ever in time and in eternity!
Amen.

Blessed Bartolo Longo

Hail, Joseph

Hail, Joseph, image of God the Father.

Hail, Joseph, father of God the Son.

Hail, Joseph, Shrine of the Holy Spirit.

Hail, Joseph, beloved of the Blessed Trinity.

Hail, Joseph, faithful auxiliary of God's designs.

Hail, Joseph, worthy spouse of the Virgin Mother.

Hail, Joseph, father of all the faithful.

Hail, Joseph, guardian of all those who have embraced holy virginity.

Hail, Joseph, faithful observer of holy silence.

Hail, Joseph, friend of holy poverty.

Hail, Joseph, example of meekness and patience.

Hail, Joseph, mirror of humility and obedience.

You are blessed among all men.

And blessed be your eyes for all they have seen.

And blessed be your ears for what they have heard.

And blessed be your hands that have touched the incarnate Word.

And blessed be your arms that bore He who bears all things.

And blessed be the breast on which the Son of God rested sweetly.

And blessed be your heart, enflamed with the most ardent love for Him.

And blessed be the Eternal Father who has chosen you.

And blessed be the Son who loved you.

And blessed be the Holy Spirit who sanctified you.

And blessed be Mary, your Bride, who loved you tenderly as a husband and as a brother.

And blessed be the Angel who served as your guardian.

And blessed are all those who love you and bless you.

Amen.

Saint John Eudes

Remember us

Remember us, Saint Joseph, and intercede for us with your prayer to your foster-Child. Ask the Blessed Virgin, your Bride, to look kindly upon us, since che is the Mother of Him who will the Father and the Holy Spirit lives and reigns eternally.

Amen.

Saint Bernardine of Siena

Act of consecration of Italy to Saint Joseph

Saint Joseph, Spouse of Mary Most Holy, Mother of Jesus and Mother of humanity, who wanted our Italy to be scattered with sanctuaries, and who has always looked upon her with the same love of predilection with which Jesus looked upon her, who wanted it to be the permanent seat of his Vicar on earth, the Pope: to you, today, we consecrate and entrust this beloved Italy and her families.

Guard her, defend her, protect her!

May the faith be pure;

may the Pastors be holy;

may vocations be abundant;

may life be sacred and defended;

may customs be sound;

may families be ordered;

may schools be Christian;

may rulers be enlightened;

may love, justice and peace reign everywhere.

O provident Custodian of the Divine Family, guard, defend and protect our young people, the hope of a better world, and the elderly, the roots of our faith and teachers of life.

Obtain for us through your powerful intercession, united with that of your Most Holy Bride, new men and women who have the courage to abrogate the iniquitous laws against God and man, inherited from a sad and dark past. With your protection, O Saint Joseph, may Italy continue to be a living centre of Christian civilisation, a beacon of evangelical light to the whole world, a land of saints for the glory of the Heavenly Father and the salvation of all men.

And, just as you once saved from the Child Jesus from mortal danger, so defend the Holy Church of God and the faith of our families from all the dark snares of evil. Jesus, Joseph and Mary, bless, protect and save Italy! Return with your help and "by your intercession" to throw open the doors to Christ.

Amen.

Stefano Lamera

O *sweet Joseph*

O sweet Joseph,
loving Father of those who place their trust in you,
today and always I entrust myself to your Heart,
"All" of Christ Jesus and Mary.
Teach me abandonment in Providence,
the treasure of silence
the total submission and donation to God.
Fill me with your "passion" for Jesus, your "tenderness"
for Mary.
May your hand lead me in the paths of Christ,
so that I may live my baptism to the full.
Obtain for me the grace to be the consoler of those who weep,
the support of the lonely,
the guide who shows the way of the Gospel.
Protect me from the attacks of the evil one,
Be the sure shield in temptation
and welcome me forever into your Fatherly Heart
with all those who come to me for help.
especially for (...)
All things, O sweet Joseph, for the glory of the Father,
of the Son and of the Holy Spirit.
Amen.

O *Saint Joseph*

O Saint Joseph, whose protection
is so great and so strong,
so immediate before the throne of God,
I place all my desires in you.
O Saint Joseph, assist me in your powerful intercession
and obtain for me all spiritual blessings
through your adopted son, Jesus Christ our Lord,
so that, having surrendered myself to your earthly power,
I may offer you my thanks and homage.
O Saint Joseph, I never tire of contemplating you
and Jesus sleeping in your arms,
I dare not approach you while He rests close
to your heart.
Hold him close in my name and kiss His tender head
for me and ask Him to return this kiss
when I draw my last breath.
Amen.

Prayer to Saint Joseph, patron of the Universal Church

O blessed Joseph, whom God has chosen to bear the name and assume the role of father in the eyes of Jesus, you who were given by Him as the pure spouse of Mary, ever Virgin, and as head of the Holy Family on earth, you whom the Vicar of Christ has chosen as the Patron and Advocate of the Universal Church, founded by Christ Himself, with the greatest possible confidence I implore of you your most powerful help for this very Church that struggles on earth.

I beg you, protect the Roman pontiff, all the bishops and the priests joined with the Holy See of Peter, with special solicitude and with your ardent, truly paternal love.

Be the defender of all those who suffer to save anguished souls, immersed in the adversity of this life.

Lead people to submit spontaneously to the Church, which is the absolutely necessary means to obtain salvation.

Deign to accept, most holy Joseph, the gift I give you. I devote myself entirely to you, so that you may be for me, always, a father, a protector and a guide along the path of salvation. Give me a pure heart, an ardent love for the inner life. Let me follow your footsteps, that I may address all my actions to the great glory of God, uniting them to the affections of the Divine Heart of Jesus and the Immaculate Heart of the Virgin Mary.

Lastly, pray for me, that I may participate in the peace and the glory you once knew, dying in sanctity.

Amen.

To obtain a holy life

O Joseph, chaste father of Jesus, most pure spouse of the Virgin Mary, pray for us every day, that, armed with the weapons of the Grace of Jesus, Son of God, fighting as we must in life, we may be crowned by Him in death.

Jesus, Mary and Joseph, I entrust my heart and soul to you.

Jesus, Mary, Joseph, assist me in my final battle.

Jesus, Mary, Joseph, may my soul depart in peace with you.

To obtain a special favour

O good Joseph, my tender father, faithful guardian of Jesus, chaste spouse of the Mother of God, I beseech and entreat you to present to God the Father His Son, crucified for sinners.

In the thrice-holy name of your Son Jesus, obtain for us from the Eternal Father the favour that we implore (...) Ask him for mercy for your children.

Amidst your eternal splendours, remember the sorrows of the earth; remember those who suffer, those who pray, those who weep. Through your prayers and those of your Holy Bride, Jesus answers us and justifies our hope.

Amen.

To achieve understanding in the family

Saint Joseph, Spouse of Mary, you have known family life as we do. Your mutual love is naturally directed toward the Son of God who became your son. And, like us, you had to make your love grow in the midst of joys and difficulties.

Saint Joseph, protect our family today. Help us to understand. Make sure that pride or selfishness never hurt our feelings. Make us ever more faithful to our tasks and to the rhythms of our days, and let us draw closer to the Son of God who is always alive in the hearts of all families.

Amen.

For a sick person

Merciful Saint Joseph, you are the hope of the sick, and all the power of Jesus is in your hands. Therefore, nothing is impossible for you. Listen with kindness to those who invoke you on this day because of the suffering members of the Church. We beseech thee, sweeten the afflictions of him whom we commend to thee in a special way. Give him the grace of total submission to the divine Will. But show him your goodness too, by transmitting patience to him and by restoring his health, with the grace of leading a life that is holy and completely pleasing to God.

Good Saint Joseph, do not make us pray in vain, but deign, through this new favour, to increase our trust and our gratitude towards you and towards the divine goodness. Amen.

For difficult causes

O thou who hast never been invoked in vain! Thou who art so powerful, close to God, that it has been said: "In heaven Joseph intercedes rather than pleads", tender father, be our advocate close to this divine Son whose putative father and faithful protector you have been here on earth; add to all your glories that of winning the difficult cause we entrust to you. We believe that you can grant our request by freeing us from the pains that afflict us. We firmly believe that you will deny nothing to the afflicted who implore.

Humbly prostrate at your feet, good Joseph, we implore you, have mercy on our tears; cover us with the mantle of your mercy and bless us all.

Amen.

INDEX

Prayers to Saint Joseph

CPSIA information can be obtained
at www.ICGtesting.com
Printed in the USA
BVHW091537221221
624599BV00016B/1603